Contributors

Adam Fike
Alexander Julian
Al Schnupp
Celeste Fenton
Gary C. Demack
Katherine Scherer and Eileen Bodoh
Kent V. Flowers
Raven Howell
Peter Keane
Marin
Mark Millicent
Mike Maroney
R. Katze
Richard A. Meyers
Rick Sulik
Robert E. Honig
Rolade Berthier, PhD
Ronni Robinson
Susanna Eun

Review Tales
A Book Magazine For Indie Authors

Founder & Editor in Chief: S. Jeyran Main
Publisher: Review Tales Publishing & Editing Services
Print & Distribution: Ingram Spark
Designs: Pexels
ISBN 978-1-988680-94-1 (Paperback)
ISBN 978-1-988680-93-4 (Digital)
www.jeyranmain.com
For all inquiries, please contact us directly.

Photo Credits from Pexels:
pmarius-miri-120056888-29749809
nazila-30129093
ebahir-34086213

Editor's Note

Welcome to the Fall edition of Review Tales Magazine. As the crisp autumn air settles in and the leaves turn to gold, we're thrilled to share the 11th issue with you—a celebration of stories, imagination, and the incredible community that surrounds us: our readers, contributors, and fellow book lovers. Every page is infused with the energy, curiosity, and passion that make literature such a vital part of our lives.

Inside, you'll find a vibrant collection of book reviews spanning genres, voices, and perspectives. From the latest bestsellers to hidden literary gems, our writers have poured heart and insight into each review, offering thoughtful guidance and inspiration for your next great read. Whether you're a devoted follower of fiction, a lover of non-fiction, or someone seeking fresh voices and stories, there's something here to spark your imagination.

We want to take a moment to extend our deepest thanks to our community. Your passion, engagement, and love of literature fuel this magazine and keep the pages turning. Every comment, recommendation, and shared story reminds us why books matter—and why sharing them is a joy we never tire of. You are the heartbeat of Review Tales Magazine, transforming reading from a solitary act into a shared journey of discovery and delight.

This fall, as you curl up with a favorite cup of tea, a cozy blanket, or a quiet nook by the window, we hope the reviews in this edition spark curiosity, ignite conversation, and perhaps even introduce you to an author or book you've never encountered before. In the swirl of autumn colors and the quiet moments between falling leaves, may this magazine be your companion, enriching your literary journey every step of the way.

Thank you for being part of our literary family. Here's to a season filled with stories that linger, ideas that challenge, and books that stay with us long after the last page is turned.

Jeyran Main

Warmly,
Jeyran Main
Editor-in-Chief, Review Tales Magazine

Welcome

FALL 2025 | ISSUE 11

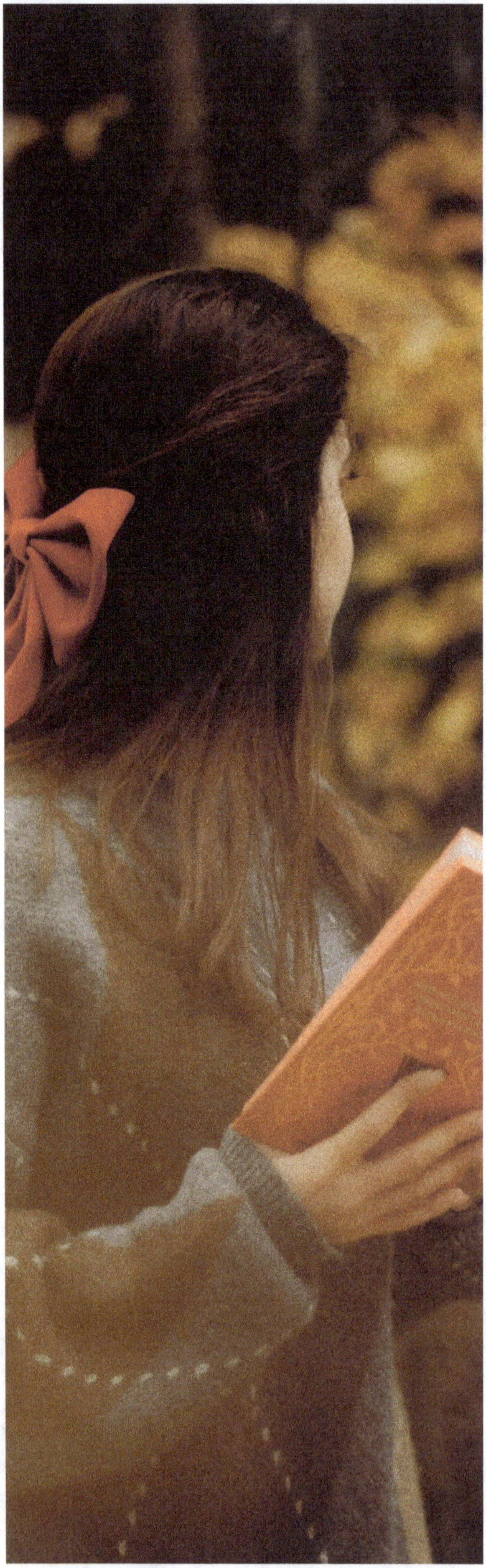

BOOK REVIEWS

Review Tales is thrilled to have reached the milestone of over 2000 book reviews. With this extensive experience, we've had the privilege of exploring a vast range of literature. Our reviews are always impartial and thoughtfully crafted to highlight authors' strengths while inspiring them to keep creating. For this fall issue, we've handpicked exceptional book reviews to feature.

TO APPLY FOR A BOOK REVIEW VISIT WWW.JEYRANMAIN.COM

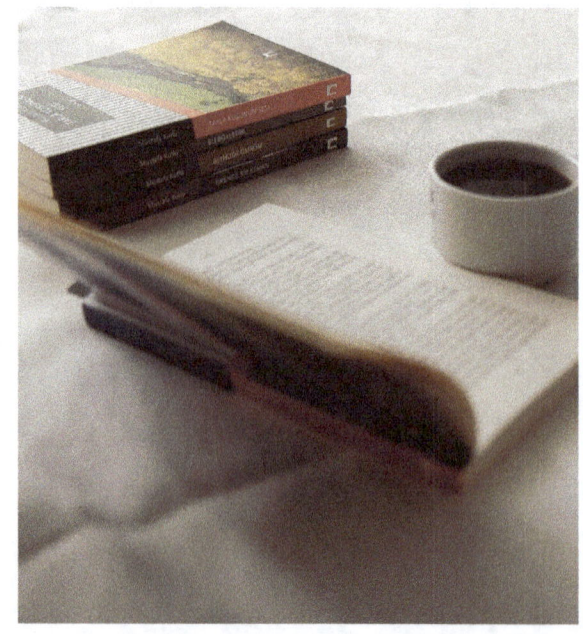

Book Reviews

THE QUIET ONES
Adam Fike

Reviewer: Jeyran Main

Adam Fike's The Quiet Ones, part of the PEOPLE MAKING DANGER series, delivers a suburban thriller that is as darkly humorous as it is suspenseful. From the very first page, Fike immerses readers in a world where ordinary neighborhoods harbor extraordinary dangers, blending tension, wit, and unexpected twists in a way that makes the story feel cinematic.

The narrative follows the disappearance of a young girl, a seemingly straightforward event that quickly unravels the lives of the surrounding families. Fike expertly captures the fragility of suburban life, illustrating how tragedy can either tear communities apart or forge unusual alliances. The twist here — neighbors finding unexpected camaraderie through the guidance of a "friendly" local serial killer — is audacious, morally complex, and darkly entertaining. It is this daring premise that sets The Quiet Ones apart from typical thriller fare.

One of the novel's strongest elements is its pacing. Fike writes in a brisk, present-tense style that mirrors the urgency of a screenplay, making the story feel like a movie playing out in real time. Each act is sharply defined, with suspense building steadily and surprises arriving when least expected. The author's skillful use of dark humor lightens the tension without undercutting the stakes, giving the story a unique voice that balances horror and levity in an uncommon but effective way.

Characterization is another highlight. While the plot is fast-moving, Fike ensures that the inhabitants of this suburban world feel distinct and memorable. From anxious parents to morally ambiguous neighbors, each character contributes to the story's nuanced examination of fear, trust, and human behavior under pressure. The serial killer, though an unconventional guide, is written with a blend of charisma and menace that keeps readers on edge while also prompting reflection on the nature of evil and complicity.

Overall, The Quiet Ones is a fast-paced, clever, and highly readable thriller that will appeal to fans of dark humor and suspense alike. Adam Fike proves himself adept at turning ordinary settings into grounds for extraordinary tension, crafting stories that entertain while keeping readers on the edge of their seats. For those looking for a suburban thriller with a cinematic feel and a morally daring twist, this book is not to be missed.

CLIMBERS
Alexander Julian

Reviewer: Jeyran Main

In Climbers, Alexander Julian constructs a post-apocalyptic world that is both hauntingly beautiful and terrifyingly unforgiving. Generations after civilization's fall, survivors cling to life atop the ruins of the Eiffel Tower, bound by rigid traditions that exile the mutated and the different. At the heart of this gripping tale is Nanky, a feral, tailed girl whose precarious position on the edge of exile forces her into a dangerous journey that challenges not only her survival instincts but the moral compass of her entire tribe.

Julian's world-building is remarkable. The ruined city of Paris, overgrown and reclaimed by nature, serves as both a stunning backdrop and a narrative force. From the remnants of Notre Dame to the perilous heights of the Tower itself, the environment pulses with danger and wonder. The author's attention to detail brings this dystopian vision to life, making the setting feel immersive, immediate, and almost cinematic.

The story excels in tension and pacing. As Nanky joins a small scouting party to search for food, the stakes escalate quickly. Encounters with monstrous creatures and the looming presence of a towering, conjoined mutant duo heighten the suspense, keeping readers on edge. Yet, the novel is more than just thrilling action; it poses profound questions about humanity, morality, and the nature of "monsters." The introduction of the peaceful, mutant-like "Saved" in the ruins challenges both the tribe and the reader to reconsider assumptions about difference, fear, and empathy.

Characterization is another of Julian's strengths. Nanky is compelling not only for her feral instincts but for the gradual emergence of her awareness, courage, and moral reasoning. The interactions among the scouting party members reveal human fragility and resilience, while the mutants—strikingly human in their own ways—provide a thought-provoking mirror for the tribe's rigid social codes.

Illustrator Devin Maupin adds depth to Julian's narrative with evocative imagery that complements the story's tone, heightening the sense of scale, danger, and post-apocalyptic wonder.

Overall, Climbers is a thrilling, thought-provoking, and visually striking novel that blends suspense, adventure, and ethical dilemmas in a uniquely post-apocalyptic setting. Julian's tale asks readers to look beyond appearances, question what it means to survive, and consider the humanity within those we might fear.

5

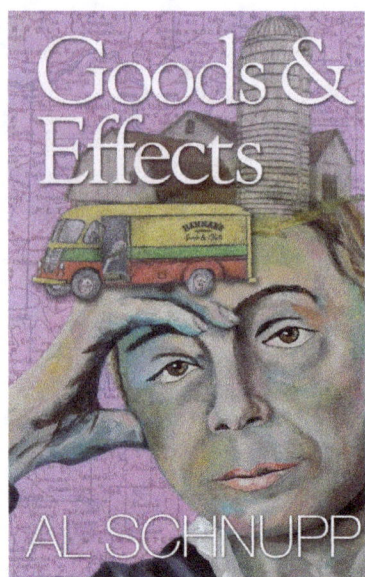

GOODS & EFFECTS
Al Schnupp

Reviewer: Jeyran Main

Al Schnupp's Goods & Effects is a profoundly human and character-driven narrative that explores grief, resilience, and the intricate web of community. At the heart of the story is Hannah Mercer, a woman devastated by the loss of her husband and sons. In response to her tragedy, Hannah sells the family farm and transforms a delivery truck into a mobile store and home, setting out on a journey that will touch lives and challenge societal norms.

The novel thrives on its rich cast of characters, each of whom is vividly drawn and deeply layered. Nathan, the motel owner, provides stability and occasional guidance; Darla, a young deaf artist, brings freshness and courage to the narrative; Wanda, the ambitious receptionist, embodies aspiration and determination; Naomi's secret desires confront rigid religious structures; and LeRoy's struggles against racial injustice add profound social commentary. Even minor characters, such as Velma, the woodworking shop owner, and the elegant librarian Vivian, contribute to the tapestry of human connection that Hannah navigates.

Schnupp's storytelling excels in balancing tragedy with warmth and humor. The writing is reflective and observant, capturing both the small, tender moments of everyday life and the broader ethical and emotional dilemmas the characters face. Hannah herself is a compelling protagonist: clever, resourceful, and morally complex. She is simultaneously a problem-solver, a schemer, and an advocate for justice, embodying both vulnerability and resilience. Through her interactions, readers witness the expansion of her understanding of humanity, even as her personal faith diminishes.

The novel's structure — a series of interconnected stories and relationships — mirrors the rhythms of a traveling community, emphasizing how individual lives intersect and influence one another. Schnupp deftly explores themes of loss, love, ambition, and social inequity, creating a narrative that feels both intimate and expansive.

Goods & Effects is ultimately a celebration of human resilience and connection. It's a book that invites readers to reflect on how tragedy, compassion, and personal courage can shape lives, foster communities, and reveal the complexities of the human spirit. Schnupp's novel is a moving, thought-provoking read, filled with memorable characters whose stories linger long after the final page.

LOST HEART IN KING MANOR
Celeste Fenton

Reviewer: Jeyran Main

Celeste Fenton's Lost Heart in King Manor, the first installment in the Mysteries of a Heart series, masterfully blends slow-burn romantic suspense with cozy mystery elements, delivering a story that is both thrilling and emotionally engaging. Set on the picturesque Dost Island, the novel introduces readers to Gabby Heart, a 45-year-old art teacher and owner of the village gift shop, who seeks nothing more than quiet days and a respite from her past. However, Gabby's plans are swiftly upended when her mother suffers a sudden health crisis, drawing her into the enigmatic King Manor and the secrets it conceals.

Fenton excels in crafting a layered narrative where danger and romance unfold simultaneously. As strange incidents escalate within the sprawling estate, a hurricane traps Gabby inside King Manor, heightening tension and creating a claustrophobic sense of urgency. Readers are kept on edge as Gabby navigates an environment rife with deception, forced to work alongside two men who may harbor motives far more sinister than they initially reveal. The interplay between suspense and romantic tension is handled deftly, making every revelation feel both surprising and inevitable.

Characterization is one of Fenton's strongest suits. Gabby is a compelling protagonist: smart, resilient, and deeply human, striking a balance between courage and vulnerability. Her relationships with the men in the story are nuanced, layered with intrigue, flirtation, and the ever-present danger that keeps the reader guessing. Supporting characters, from the quirky village locals to the mysterious figures within King Manor, add depth, humor, and emotional texture, enriching the narrative.

The novel's setting also deserves praise. Fenton vividly captures the charm of a seaside village juxtaposed against the eerie grandeur of a centuries-old estate, enhancing both the cozy and suspenseful elements of the story. Her writing is immersive, blending mystery, humor, and romance seamlessly, which makes the novel feel cinematic in its pacing and tension.

Lost Heart in King Manor is a captivating start to the Mysteries of a Heart series, ideal for fans of strong female protagonists, layered romantic suspense, and small-town mysteries hiding dark truths. With its slow-burning tension, clever twists, and richly drawn characters, Fenton delivers a story that is impossible to put down.

THE BROKEN FIFE
Gary C. Demack

Reviewer: Jeyran Main

Gary C. Demack's The Broken Fife is a sweeping Civil War-era tale that seamlessly weaves together love, loss, and the transcendent power of music. At its heart is Junius Hart, a young man whose life is irrevocably changed by love and war. Junius falls deeply in love with Ruby, an enslaved woman on his father's farm, and their tentative bid for freedom through the Underground Railroad sets the stage for a story that is as emotionally stirring as it is historically rich.

Demack's narrative excels in blending historical detail with deeply human storytelling. The novel captures the moral complexities and harsh realities of the Civil War period, from the ambushes of Jayhawkers to the stark divisions of loyalty and ideology. Junius's enlistment in the Missouri State Guard, followed by his entanglement with the Confederate Army, illustrates the difficult choices and ethical dilemmas faced by individuals caught in the tides of history. The backdrop of war is vivid, immersive, and expertly researched, giving the story a strong sense of authenticity.

Music serves as both a metaphor and a lifeline throughout the novel. Junius, a gifted fifer, uses his art to navigate grief, hope, and resilience. The recurring motif of the broken fife symbolizes loss, memory, and the enduring connection between past and present, lending the story a poignant emotional resonance. Readers are drawn into Junius's journey not just through his physical trials but through the music that accompanies his life's most significant moments.

Characterization is another strength of the book. Junius is complex and relatable, embodying courage, vulnerability, and moral reflection. Ruby's presence, though often distant, shapes his choices and motivations, while supporting characters — from fellow soldiers to strangers encountered post-war — enhance the narrative's depth and texture.

The Broken Fife is a compelling exploration of love, history, and redemption. Its intricate storytelling, evocative imagery, and richly developed characters create a narrative that lingers long after the final page. For fans of Civil War fiction, tragic romance, and historical narratives infused with moral complexity, Gary C. Demack delivers a story that is both heartbreaking and uplifting, proving the enduring power of music and the human spirit even amidst history's darkest chapters.

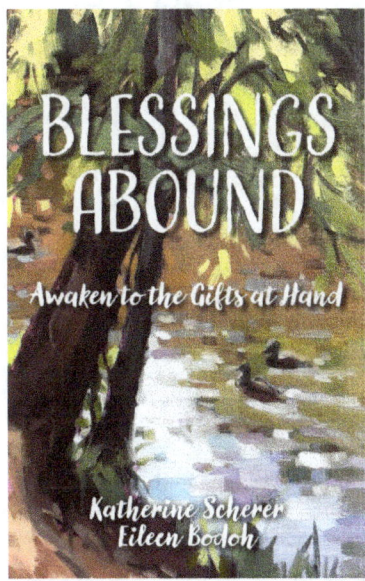

BLESSINGS ABOUND: AWAKEN TO THE GIFTS AT HAND

Katherine Scherer and Eileen Bodoh

Reviewer: Jeyran Main

Blessings Abound: Awaken to the Gifts at Hand by Katherine Scherer and Eileen Bodoh is an inspiring and insightful guide for anyone seeking to cultivate gratitude, awareness, and spiritual growth. Rooted in both ancient wisdom and contemporary reflections, the book serves as a gentle yet profound roadmap for recognizing the abundance in everyday life and deepening one's connection to the divine.

The authors draw upon a diverse tapestry of sources, from Native American traditions and the Christian Bible to literary luminaries such as Wordsworth, Thoreau, Whitman, and Tagore. This eclectic approach enriches the text, offering readers multiple perspectives on the themes of blessings, mindfulness, and spiritual awakening. Scherer and Bodoh skillfully weave these influences together, creating a narrative that is both accessible and deeply thought-provoking.

Central to the book is the concept of awareness — learning to notice and appreciate both the ordinary and extraordinary gifts present in daily life. The authors guide readers through exercises, reflections, and meditative practices designed to help uncover hidden blessings, amplify their significance, and integrate gratitude into practical living. Each chapter offers actionable insights alongside reflective wisdom, making it ideal for readers who are both contemplative and action-oriented.

The writing is warm, encouraging, and poetic, imbuing the text with a sense of serenity and inspiration. Readers are invited to slow down, reconnect with their inner selves, and embrace the magic inherent in life's moments. The book's tone is inclusive and uplifting, appealing to a broad audience regardless of faith tradition, while honoring the spiritual and cultural roots from which it draws its inspiration.

Blessings Abound is more than just a guide; it is a companion for anyone seeking to live a life of greater awareness, gratitude, and joy. Scherer and Bodoh remind readers that blessings are all around us, waiting to be recognized and cherished, and that cultivating a mindset of gratitude is a transformative practice that can enrich every aspect of life.

UNION RULES
Kent V. Flowers

Reviewer: Jeyran Main

Kent V. Flowers' Union Rules is a gripping science fiction tale that explores intelligence, power, and rebellion in a harsh industrial universe. Set on Planet Cold Blue, a factory world dominated by city-sized production facilities, the story follows Arlin, a guard whose life is irrevocably changed when an unmanned observation craft from the Builders' planet abducts him and grants him super intelligence along with vast knowledge. What the Builders expect in return, however, sets the stage for interplanetary intrigue and a revolution that challenges the very foundations of this tightly controlled society.

Flowers' world-building is intricate and immersive. Planet Cold Blue is vividly depicted as a place where most of the population lives and works within the factory. In contrast, others, including natives and exiled prisoners, inhabit the harsh outside. The factory operates under strict Union management, with complex hierarchies and strict labor expectations, reflecting real-world social and labor dynamics through a futuristic lens. The author skillfully uses these elements to create a tension-filled backdrop where morality, power, and survival collide.

The narrative excels in exploring themes of loyalty, exploitation, and resistance. Arlin's character development is compelling: initially indifferent to the origins of the workers, he evolves as the story progresses, forced to confront ethical dilemmas and his role in the exploitation of others. The tension escalates as workers resist enslavement, leading to a full-scale rebellion that questions not only Arlin's loyalty but the nature of justice and leadership under oppressive regimes.

Union Rules also stands out for its fast-paced plotting and suspenseful sequences. Flowers combines political intrigue, sci-fi concepts, and high-stakes conflict to create a story that keeps readers engaged from start to finish. The novel's moral complexity, layered world-building, and vivid descriptions of the factory society make it both thought-provoking and entertaining.

Overall, Union Rules is a compelling addition to the sci-fi genre for readers who enjoy futuristic societies, ethical dilemmas, and rebellion against oppressive systems. Kent V. Flowers delivers a story that is intellectually stimulating, action-packed, and morally challenging, proving that even in a universe dominated by machines and control, the human—or sentient—spirit fights to remain free.

HEDGEHOG'S WINTER
Raven Howell

Reviewer: Jeyran Main

Raven Howell's Hedgehog's Winter is a heartwarming, enchanting children's story that perfectly captures the magic and wonder of the winter season. Ideal for young readers, the book follows Hedgehog as he eagerly anticipates the joys of snow — building a snowman, skating on ice, and sledding down hills — while discovering the importance of curiosity, friendship, and perseverance along the way. Through gentle storytelling, Howell encourages children to explore the small wonders in their world, celebrate creativity, and appreciate the joy that comes from connecting with others.

The story begins with Hedgehog brimming with excitement for winter activities, only to find that his usual friends — Bear, Raccoon, and Chipmunk — are already preparing for hibernation. Determined not to let this stop him, Hedgehog sets out in search of a companion for his seasonal adventures. Along the way, he meets Deer, and together they embark on a series of joyful winter activities, from ice skating to building a snowman and even fashioning a makeshift sled from a piece of bark. These shared experiences highlight cooperation, creativity, and the joy of discovering companionship in unexpected places.

Howell's prose is gentle, rhythmic, and highly accessible, making Hedgehog's Winter a perfect read-aloud story for parents and children. The narrative captures both the excitement and reflective moments of winter, inviting readers to immerse themselves in Hedgehog's experiences and to notice the beauty in small details — such as his curiosity about the taste of a falling snowflake. The story strikes a balance between playful energy and tender, reflective passages, allowing young readers to connect emotionally with the protagonist.

The illustrations enhance Howell's story beautifully, bringing the forest and its inhabitants to life with warmth, charm, and vivid detail. They capture the textures of snow, the expressive faces of the animals, and the gentle magic that infuses Hedgehog's world. Each image complements the text harmoniously to create a fully immersive experience that delights the senses and sparks the imagination.

The book concludes with Hedgehog returning to his cozy burrow, tired but happy, as he reflects on the simple joys of his winter adventure. Hedgehog's Winter is a delightful, comforting story that celebrates curiosity, imagination, and the value of friendship, making it a must-read for children and families seeking a magical and heartwarming tale during the colder months.

PROXIMA'S GIFT
Peter Keane

Reviewer: Jeyran Main

Marc Peter Keane's Proxima's Gift is a mesmerizing work of speculative fiction that fuses post-apocalyptic survival, philosophical exploration, and deep ecological awareness into a lyrical narrative. Set three centuries after a solar cataclysm decimates much of the human population, the story centers on the Children of Proxima, a group living in the remote mountains of Japan who have developed a unique organ that grants them a sixth sense: empathy, or the "glow." This extraordinary ability allows them to connect with all living beings, sensing their emotions, intentions, and presence.

The protagonist, Azami, struggles to control her heightened empathy. Unlike her peers, she risks being overwhelmed by the collective consciousness around her, and the only way to survive—and to gain wisdom and power—is to dissolve herself fully into the natural world. Through this journey, Keane explores profound questions of identity, morality, and the delicate balance between human ambition and environmental harmony. Azami's personal journey is at once thrilling and deeply introspective, as readers are invited to experience the world through countless perspectives and reflect on the interconnectedness of life.

Keane's prose is lush, deliberate, and highly visual, drawing on his decades of experience as a Japanese garden designer to craft landscapes that are vivid, layered, and almost spiritual in their resonance. From snowmelt rivers and budding fields to minute movements of insects, his attention to detail transforms the natural world into a character in its own right. The story is as much about place as it is about people, and the seamless blending of natural observation with speculative narrative gives the book a meditative, immersive quality.

Proxima's Gift is also notable for its philosophical depth. Keane interrogates the consequences of absolute empathy and the moral dilemmas it creates. Should one accept power if it alienates them from society? What does it mean to be human when one can feel the entirety of life around them? These questions drive the narrative forward, ensuring that the book resonates long after the final page.

For readers of speculative fiction who crave lyrical prose, thoughtful world-building, and stories that challenge both imagination and ethics, Proxima's Gift is a remarkable achievement. Marc Peter Keane delivers a story that is inventive, reflective, and deeply human, celebrating the interconnections of life while exploring the risks and responsibilities of extraordinary abilities.

AL'S JOURNEY

Marin

Reviewer: Jeyran Main

Al's Journey by Marin is a magical and inspirational tale that seamlessly blends mythology, spirituality, and coming-of-age adventure into a story that is both heartfelt and transformative. Centered on Al, an orphan boy from a gold-digging tribe, the story follows his extraordinary quest to mature and discover his purpose under the guidance of his wise grandfather, the shaman. On his 100th birthday, the shaman sets Al on a path to the roofless sacred hut atop a mountain, a journey designed to test his courage, resilience, and insight.

The narrative is richly symbolic, portraying Al's climb as both a physical and spiritual ascent. Along the way, mystical fireflies serve as guides, illuminating the boy's path and reinforcing the novel's themes of faith, perseverance, and enlightenment. Each challenge that Al encounters is carefully crafted to test his character and provoke growth, making his journey feel both universal and deeply personal. Readers are drawn into the suspense and wonder of the trek, rooting for Al as he overcomes obstacles that require mental agility, emotional strength, and moral discernment.

Marin's storytelling is lyrical and immersive, with a cadence that evokes both ancient oral traditions and modern fantasy. The writing highlights the interplay between human striving and divine guidance, offering readers a reflective meditation on the pursuit of wisdom and the process of self-discovery. The sacred mountain, the summit hut, and the fireflies are more than mere settings or plot devices—they symbolize stages of personal growth and spiritual awakening, giving the story layers of meaning that resonate across age groups.

The climax, in which Al meets the creator and asks profound questions about the meaning of life, is both moving and thought-provoking. It illustrates how challenges, reflection, and openness to wisdom can accelerate personal development, allowing a young hero to grow mentally, emotionally, and spiritually in ways that prepare him to serve his community.

Al's Journey is a compelling and uplifting tale for readers of all ages who enjoy magical adventures, spiritual reflection, and stories of courage and growth. Marin delivers a narrative that inspires self-exploration and celebrates the transformative power of experience, making it a memorable addition to the genre of mystical coming-of-age stories.

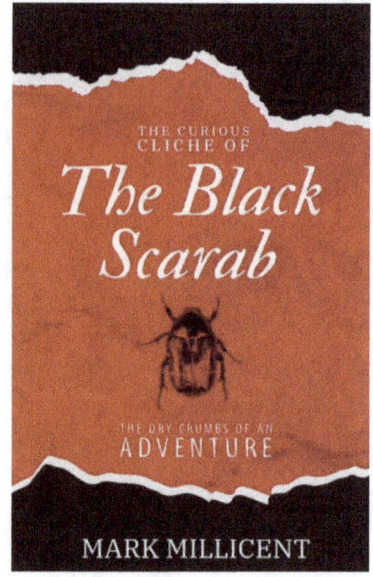

THE CURIOUS CLICHÉ OF THE BLACK SCARAB

Mark Millicent

Reviewer: Jeyran Main

Mark Millicent's The Curious Cliché of the Black Scarab is a delightfully whimsical romp through early 20th-century Egypt, blending historical adventure, slapstick humor, and absurdly entertaining capers. Set in 1912, the novel follows two inept reporters, Larry Littleton and Harry Hackney, who are improbably tasked with uncovering the tomb of the High Chantress of Asanti—and with it, a centuries-old recipe for the world's most coveted ceremonial funeral dinner crackers. From the outset, Millicent sets a playful tone, balancing historical setting with comedic absurdity to create a story that is as unpredictable as it is charming.

The narrative thrives on its fast-paced plot and outrageous scenarios. Larry and Harry bumble through London and the Nile, encountering a host of colorful characters, from undercover agents to cunning rivals, while narrowly escaping ambushes, desert treachery, and even a villainous monkey. Their rival, Singleton Sinclair, adds a layer of tension and comic villainy, culminating in a chaotic showdown that keeps readers on their toes—and laughing. Millicent's knack for combining historical detail with zany plot twists ensures that every chapter offers both entertainment and surprise.

Characterization is deliberately exaggerated and delightfully over the top. Larry and Harry are lovable for their haplessness, while Sinclair is a comically ruthless antagonist whose schemes are as elaborate as they are doomed to fail. The interactions among characters, paired with witty dialogue and clever wordplay, create an engaging and often laugh-out-loud reading experience.

The novel also impresses with its creative blending of history and humor. While Millicent captures the flavor and atmosphere of early 20th-century Egypt, he infuses it with playful anachronisms and absurdities—most notably the quest for the ceremonial crackers—that make the story feel fresh, inventive, and wholly original.

The Curious Cliché of the Black Scarab is a madcap adventure that will appeal to readers who enjoy historical fiction with a twist of comedy, clever absurdity, and fast-paced, unpredictable plots. With its memorable characters, richly imagined settings, and delightfully crunchy sense of humor, Millicent delivers a story that is impossible to put down and guaranteed to leave readers both entertained and craving more of his outrageous exploits.

LIE ME DOWN AMONG THE COLD DARK PINES

Mike Maroney

Reviewer: Jeyran Main

Mike Maroney's Lie Me Down Among the Cold Dark Pines is a gripping, darkly layered young adult thriller that delves into small-town secrets, family dysfunction, and the dangerous consequences of curiosity. The story follows Hart, a sixteen-year-old navigating a chaotic home life with her feckless mother, Nancy, and her brother Howell. When the family inherits a house in LaFayetteville, Hart anticipates stability, but the town proves as treacherous as the road she left behind.

Maroney excels in creating tension through both personal and societal conflict. Hart's life becomes intertwined with mystery and danger after she discovers the body of Jessica, a local stripper, on the mountainside. This initial shock ignites a series of revelations involving corruption, environmental negligence, and drug trafficking, drawing Hart into a deadly investigation. The author effectively layers multiple plotlines—from small-town dynamics and high school relationships to industrial conspiracies and meth operations—maintaining suspense and momentum throughout.

Hart is a compelling protagonist: determined, resourceful, and morally grounded, even when confronted with peril and betrayal. Her relationships, particularly with Brandi, her cousin, and the enigmatic Riley, reveal the complexities of trust, loyalty, and identity. Maroney also tackles sensitive themes with nuance, including transgender identity, systemic corruption, and the struggles of youth facing adult realities. The narrative does not shy away from violence or ethical ambiguity, which amplifies the stakes and immerses readers in Hart's dangerous world.

The novel's setting—the rural mountains and small-town LaFayetteville—is richly drawn, heightening the claustrophobic tension of a community rife with secrets. From chemical spills to meth labs hidden in the wilderness, Maroney blends realism with thriller elements to create an authentic, high-stakes environment.

Lie Me Down Among the Cold Dark Pines is a fast-paced, multi-layered thriller that keeps readers on edge from start to finish. With vivid characterization, intricate plotting, and a darkly suspenseful atmosphere, Maroney delivers a story that is both entertaining and thought-provoking. It is a must-read for fans of young adult mysteries and thrillers that tackle complex social issues while providing gripping suspense and action.

HEARTS ON THE LINE
R. Katze

Reviewer: Jeyran Main

R. Katze's Hearts on the Line is a heartfelt small-town romance that explores friendship, courage, and the complexities of rekindled love. The story centers on Jennifer and Adam, childhood friends whose paths diverged over the years, only to converge again under tense circumstances. Jennifer is struggling to free herself from an abusive ex, Eric, while Adam, a rising NFL star, returns home to confront personal and professional crossroads. When Adam steps in to protect Jennifer, the two friends agree to pretend they are in a relationship—a "fake dating" arrangement that serves as a shield against external threats but also rekindles dormant feelings.

The novel excels at depicting the emotional stakes of both romance and personal safety. Jennifer's vulnerability and resilience are portrayed with sensitivity, highlighting her struggle to reclaim autonomy and navigate fear. Adam's protective instincts, combined with his internal conflicts about career and love, create a compelling slow-burn romance that balances tension, tenderness, and genuine emotional growth. The dynamic between the two characters is both realistic and engaging, with chemistry that evolves naturally as they confront challenges together.

R. Katze effectively blends romance with suspense, keeping readers invested in the story's dual arcs: the development of Jennifer and Adam's relationship and the looming threat posed by Eric. The small-town setting adds intimacy and charm, while also emphasizing the stakes of secrecy, reputation, and trust. Readers are drawn into the narrative by a combination of relatable characters, high emotional stakes, and moments of heartfelt connection.

While the plot is familiar within the friends-to-lovers and fake-dating subgenres, Hearts on the Line stands out due to its focus on personal courage, the emotional realism of its protagonists, and the slow, satisfying progression of their relationship. It is a story that celebrates second chances, loyalty, and the courage to confront both past trauma and future possibilities.

Hearts on the Line is a compelling read for fans of contemporary romance, particularly those who enjoy small-town settings, protective heroes, and slow-burn friends-to-lovers stories. With its blend of suspense, heartfelt emotion, and romance, R. Katze delivers a narrative that is engaging, tender, and emotionally resonant.

15

THE HALF-FULL-GLASS USER'S MANUAL
Richard A. Meyers

Reviewer: Jeyran Main

Richard A. Meyers' The Half-Full-Glass User's Manual is a whimsical and reflective guide to living with more joy, balance, and awareness. Purportedly discovered in a dusty attic as the last surviving piece of a mysterious 1920s "Starter Kit," the book blends humor, insight, and ceremonial mischief into a unique manual for intentional living. With outrageous wordplay, ludicrous anecdotes, and playful exercises, Meyers invites readers to explore gratitude, humility, and self-awareness through a lens that is both lighthearted and deeply philosophical.

The manual stands out for its inventive approach. Unlike traditional self-help books, Meyers employs humor and whimsy to convey serious concepts about living intentionally. Each page encourages readers to pause, reflect, and experiment with new ways of seeing the world. The ceremonial mischief and wordplay add charm and accessibility, ensuring that readers engage with the material joyfully rather than feeling instructed or lectured. This blend of levity and wisdom is ideal for those seeking personal growth without the weight of rigid methodologies.

The book also serves as a meditation on the creative and emotional journey of authorship. Meyers' narrative invites readers into the playful, often unpredictable process of making meaning, whether through ritual, reflection, or storytelling. The manual subtly encourages readers to embrace curiosity, cultivate mindfulness, and celebrate the ordinary moments that are often overlooked.

With a November 11 launch, The Half-Full-Glass User's Manual is perfectly timed for readers seeking a fresh perspective on intentional living. Its combination of humor, wisdom, and interactive exercises makes it a standout in contemporary self-help and lifestyle literature. Whether readers approach it as a reflective guide, a conversation starter, or simply an entertaining read, Meyers' manual offers both inspiration and delight.

The Half-Full-Glass User's Manual is a charming, unconventional, and thoughtful guide for anyone interested in exploring joy, mindfulness, and gratitude in playful yet meaningful ways. Richard A. Meyers delivers a book that is as entertaining as it is enlightening, reminding us that sometimes, the simplest insights arrive in the most unexpected packages.

DEATH UNMASKED
Rick Sulik

Reviewer: Jeyran Main

Rick Sulik's Death Unmasked is a gripping police thriller that fuses suspense, mystery, and metaphysical elements into a unique and compelling narrative. Written by a thirty-nine-year veteran of law enforcement, the book draws upon Sulik's extensive experience to create authentic investigative scenarios, while integrating karma, psychic abilities, remote viewing, and out-of-body experiences to elevate the story beyond conventional crime fiction.

The novel follows Houston Homicide Detective Sean Jamison as he hunts a chilling serial killer who stalks women throughout the city. Each murder is accompanied by a cryptic quotation from Oscar Wilde's The Ballad of Reading Gaol, adding an eerie, literary texture to the unfolding horror. As Jamison investigates, he is confronted not only with the present-day murders but with fragments of his own past lives, which reveal the woman he lost and the karmic entanglements that echo across time. Sulik's incorporation of reincarnation and psychic phenomena adds a layer of complexity and intrigue, transforming the narrative into both a murder mystery and a metaphysical exploration.

One of the novel's standout features is Sulik's attention to detail. His police procedural knowledge lends realism to crime scene investigations, interviews, and forensic analysis. At the same time, the author's vivid descriptions of Houston's streets, flea markets, and neighborhoods ground the supernatural elements in a tangible setting. This juxtaposition of the ordinary and the extraordinary heightens suspense and engages readers on multiple levels.

Sulik's protagonist, Sean Jamison, is both relatable and multifaceted. Jamison's struggle to reconcile his present life with memories of past existences adds emotional depth and personal stakes to the hunt for the killer. Readers are drawn into his psychological and spiritual journey, creating a thriller that is both cerebral and action-packed.

Death Unmasked is an ambitious and inventive work for fans of crime thrillers with a metaphysical twist. Its combination of suspense, psychic phenomena, and literary intrigue ensures an engaging and thought-provoking experience from start to finish. Sulik's novel is perfect for readers who enjoy mysteries that challenge the boundaries of time, perception, and the human psyche.

AFTERMATH BOY
Robert E. Hong

Reviewer: Jeyran Main

Robert E. Honig's Aftermath Boy is a powerful, multi-generational novel that explores Holocaust survival, inherited trauma, and the complex landscape of postwar American life. Told through alternating perspectives and timelines, the story follows Rozsa, a Hungarian Jewish survivor, and her son Billy, a "child of the Holocaust", grappling with personal and societal disillusionment decades later. From the harrowing death marches and concentration camps Rozsa endures to Billy's surreal legal and existential struggles in contemporary America, Honig weaves history, memory, and moral inquiry into a deeply affecting narrative.

Rozsa's chapters are vividly immersive. Her first-person accounts capture the brutality of fascist Europe while portraying her resilience, pragmatism, and maternal depth. Relationships with her sisters and father add layers of emotional complexity, painting a rich portrait of familial bonds tested under extreme circumstances. Billy's chapters, by contrast, confront the lingering effects of inherited trauma, exploring postwar identity, survivor guilt, and the anxieties of navigating modern American bureaucracy, including a surreal FBI raid under the Patriot Act. Honig skillfully parallels historical oppression with contemporary challenges, demonstrating how trauma echoes across generations.

Honig's prose is literary and evocative, balancing lyrical reflection with black humor and philosophical insight. The narrative structure, while ambitious, is handled with precision, seamlessly interweaving multiple timelines and voices. Themes of Jewish identity, authoritarianism, and moral ambiguity resonate throughout, illustrating how personal and political histories intertwine. Tonal shifts—from mournful to satirical—enhance the narrative, underscoring the absurdities and tragedies of both past and present.

The book stands out for its emotional depth, historical clarity, and contemporary relevance. Readers who appreciated works like Maus by Art Spiegelman, Everything Is Illuminated by Jonathan Safran Foer, or Julie Orringer's The Invisible Bridge will find a similarly moving experience here. Honig delivers a story that is both urgent and timeless, a meditation on memory, moral reckoning, and the enduring power of love and resilience.

Aftermath Boy is not merely a Holocaust story—it is an exploration of legacy, identity, and how history continues to shape lives. With its haunting narrative and profound emotional resonance, Honig's novel lingers long after the final page, offering both illumination and reckoning.

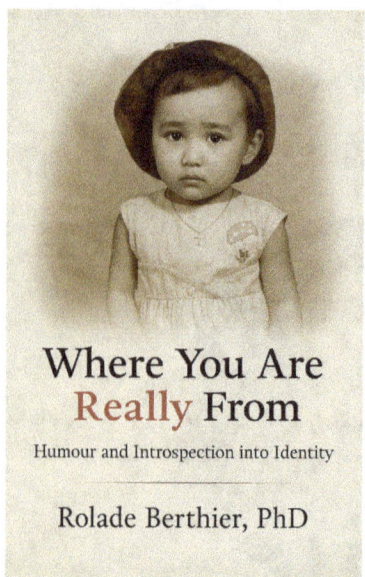

WHERE YOU ARE REALLY FROM
Rolade Berthier, PhD

Reviewer: Jeyran Main

Rolade Berthier's Where You Are Really From is an insightful, witty, and thought-provoking exploration of identity, belonging, and the subtle ways everyday questions can reveal assumptions about culture, ethnicity, and nationality. At its core, the book examines the deceptively simple query "Where are you really from?"—a question that can spark curiosity, connection, or discomfort —and traces its implications across social interactions and lived experiences.

Berthier blends analysis, humor, and personal narrative to illuminate the multifaceted nature of this common yet complex question. Through lively chapters, the book examines how names, accents, passports, family histories, and cultural representation complicate notions of origin. The author balances critical reflection with playful observation, highlighting both the persistence of stereotypes and the resilience of those who navigate these encounters. By examining contexts across countries including Australia, Canada, France, Luxembourg, Poland, the Republic of Ireland, Singapore, the Philippines, the UK, and the USA, Berthier emphasizes that this question—and the assumptions behind it—transcends borders.

The book also expands into broader discussions of global upbringing, ethnic humor, and even the role of artificial intelligence in contemporary identity discourse. Appendices offer targeted reflections on belonging, language use, and ethnicism in the 21st century, providing readers with practical and thought-provoking insights into everyday cultural interactions. Berthier's writing is accessible, engaging, and often humorous, making complex social dynamics understandable without losing nuance or depth.

Where You Are Really From excels in its ability to provoke reflection while entertaining readers. It challenges audiences to consider how questions about origin can unintentionally reinforce biases or assumptions, and encourages more mindful, respectful conversations about identity. The book's combination of research, lived experience, and humor creates a compelling, layered narrative that resonates with readers of diverse backgrounds.

Berthier's work is both educational and enjoyable, emphasizing that behind the seemingly innocuous question "Where are you really from?" lies an opportunity for meaningful dialogue about respect, inclusion, and human connection. This book is a valuable read for anyone interested in culture, identity, and social interaction in a globalized world.

OUT OF THE PANTRY: A DISORDERED EATING JOURNEY
Ronni Robinson

Reviewer: Jeyran Main

Ronni Robinson's Out of the Pantry: A Disordered Eating Journey is a raw, candid, and ultimately empowering memoir that chronicles one woman's decades-long struggle with compulsive overeating. From pre-teen childhood binges to adult life, Robinson offers an unflinching look at the pervasive thoughts, shame, and heartbreak that accompany living with a disordered relationship with food. Her journey is not only a personal story but also a universal exploration of resilience, self-discovery, and the pursuit of healing.

The narrative begins in Robinson's suburban childhood, where seemingly minor events—such as her mother hiding cookies—trigger compulsive eating behaviors that escalate over the years. Robinson candidly recounts experiences that many may find uncomfortable, including secretive binges, stealing food, eating from others' plates, and scavenging from the trash. These moments are described with honesty and clarity, providing readers with an intimate understanding of the compulsive mind and the profound isolation it can create.

What sets Robinson's memoir apart is her transformation from a life of secrecy and shame to one of awareness and empowerment. The turning point arrives when she hears the term "compulsive overeater" on television. This moment reframes her experiences as a recognized mental illness, a disease rather than a personal failing. From there, Robinson embarks on a path of active recovery, attending therapy, joining Overeaters Anonymous, reading extensively, and even blogging anonymously to process her journey. Her story demonstrates that knowledge, support, and perseverance can transform a life once controlled by compulsion into one guided by choice and self-compassion.

Robinson's writing is both brutally honest and deeply empathetic. She balances pain and struggle with moments of insight, reflection, and hope, creating a narrative that resonates emotionally without becoming didactic. Readers are invited not only to witness her journey but also to find inspiration in her courage and determination to reclaim her life.

Out of the Pantry is essential reading for anyone seeking to understand disordered eating, mental health, and personal resilience. Robinson's memoir offers a poignant, insightful, and inspiring exploration of living fully despite the long shadow of compulsive behaviors.

20

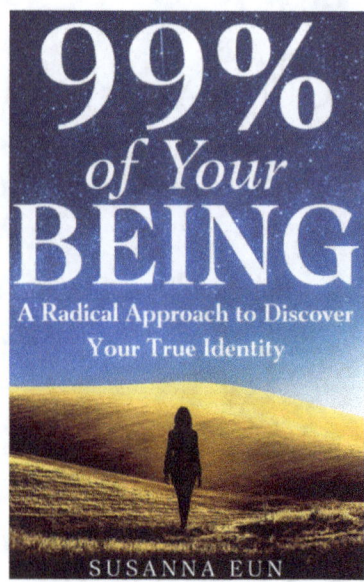

99% OF YOUR BEING
Susanna Eun

Reviewer: Jeyran Main

In 99% of Your Being: A Transformative Journey to Your True Self, Susanna Eun offers a profound and practical roadmap for self-discovery, inner peace, and spiritual awakening. Eun challenges the common notion that personal growth requires constant effort to "fix" oneself. Instead, she posits that most of us operate from only 1% of our potential—our anxious, reactive ego-mind—while the remaining 99% of our being, a vast conscious presence, remains largely untapped, waiting to be awakened.

The book blends timeless non-dual teachings, Buddhist wisdom, and holistic medicine to create a framework that is both accessible and profoundly transformative. Eun guides readers on a journey of awareness, helping them disengage from fear, overthinking, and stress, and access the calm, expansive presence that is inherent within. Her guidance is enriched with practical exercises, reflective prompts, and real-world examples, ensuring that readers can integrate spiritual principles into daily life without feeling abstract or inaccessible.

Eun's writing is compassionate, clear, and empowering. She addresses the modern struggle with anxiety, self-doubt, and disconnection, demonstrating how these challenges arise from operating primarily in the reactive ego-mind. Through her teachings, readers are invited to cultivate mindfulness, presence, and self-compassion, learning to live from a more authentic and conscious part of themselves.

One of the book's key strengths is its balance between theory and practice. It not only explores the philosophy behind spiritual awakening but also provides concrete steps for meditation, energetic alignment, and mindful living. These tools help readers develop emotional resilience, deepen their awareness, and build stronger connections with themselves and the world around them.

99% of Your Being is ideal for anyone seeking a path beyond conventional self-help or productivity guides. It is a gentle yet powerful reminder that lasting peace, creativity, and clarity are not distant goals but qualities already present within us. Eun's approach encourages readers to awaken their untapped potential and embrace a life rooted in awareness, authenticity, and inner freedom.

This book is a transformative guide to self-discovery, providing both insightful perspectives and practical guidance. For those ready to move beyond the limitations of the ego-mind and awaken the vast potential within, 99% of Your Being is an essential read.